SCHIRMER'S LIBRARY OF MUSICAL CLASSICS

PETER I. TCHAIKOVSKY

Op. 71a

The Nutcracker Suite

Miniature Overture
March
Dance of the Candy Fairy
Russian Dance, "Trepak"
Arab Dance
Chinese Dance
Dance of the Reed-Flutes
Waltz of the Flowers

Library Vol. 1359
Arranged for Piano, Four-Hands by
E. LANGER
Edited by
CONSTANTIN STERNBERG

Library Vol. 1447
Arranged for Piano Solo by
STEPÁN ESIPOFF
Edited by
CARL DEIS

G. SCHIRMER, Inc.

DISTRIBUTED BY

HAL•LEONARD®
CORPORATION
7777 W. BLUEMOUND RD. P.O. BOX 13819 MILWAUKEE, WI 53213

SUITE

For Full Orchestra
Selected from the music of the ballet

"The Nutcracker"

by
P. TCHAIKOVSKY

Miniature Overture

Edited by
Constantin Sternberg

Arranged for 4 hands by
E. Langer

SECONDO

SUITE
For Full Orchestra
Selected from the music of the ballet
"The Nutcracker"
by
P. TCHAIKOVSKY

Miniature Overture

Edited by
Constantin Sternberg

Arranged for 4 hands by
E. Langer

PRIMO

(l.h. under)

3

SECONDO

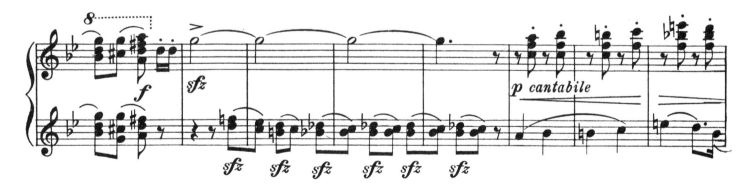

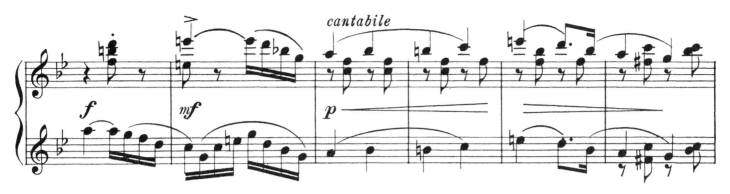

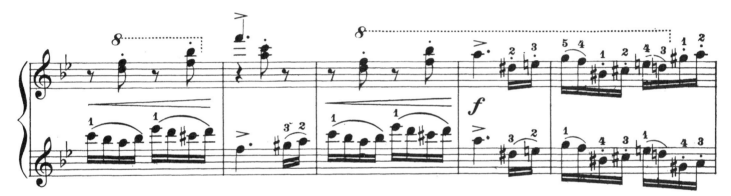

SECONDO

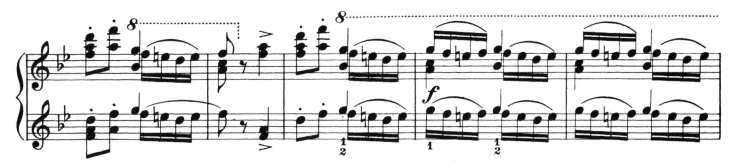

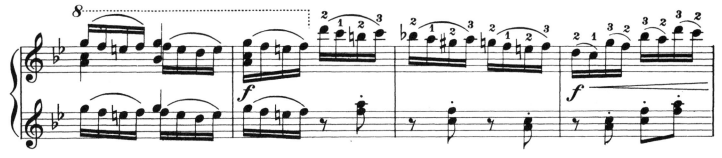

SECONDO

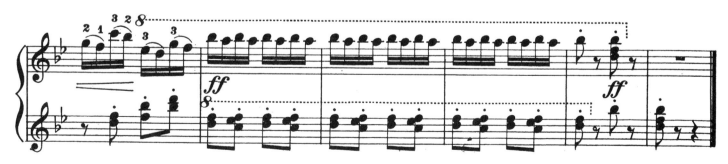

March

SECONDO

Tempo di Marcia vivo (♩ = 144)

March

SECONDO

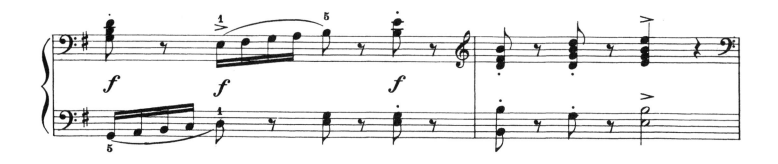

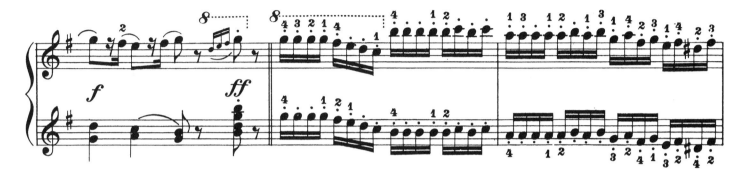

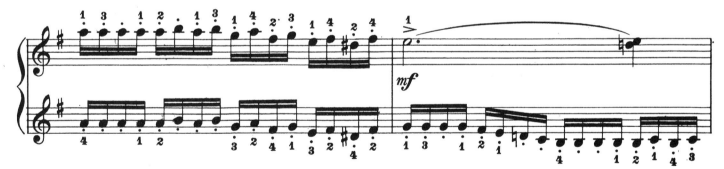

(over)

SECONDO

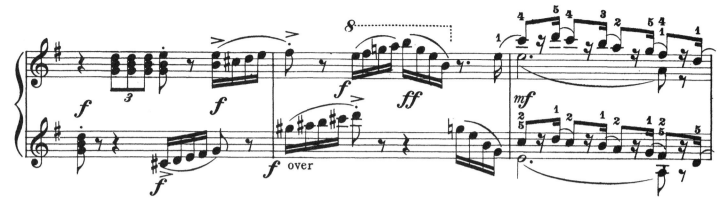

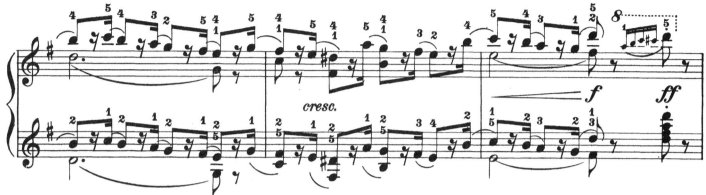

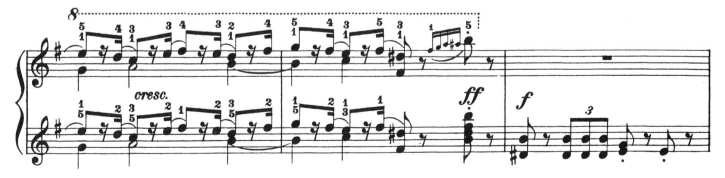

SECONDO

(vide ossia)

Dance of the Candy Fairy

SECONDO

Dance of the Candy Fairy

PRIMO

SECONDO

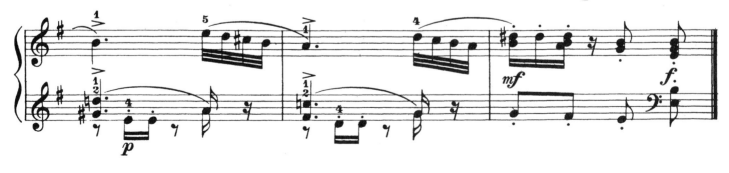

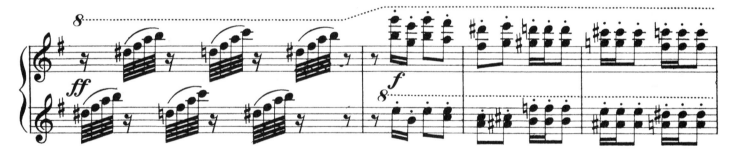

Russian Dance, "Trépak"

SECONDO

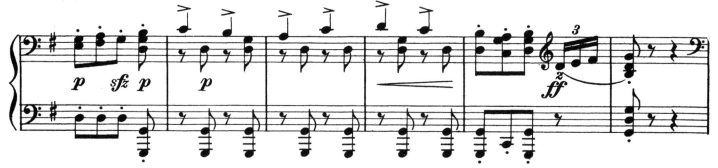

Russian Dance, "Trépak"

PRIMO

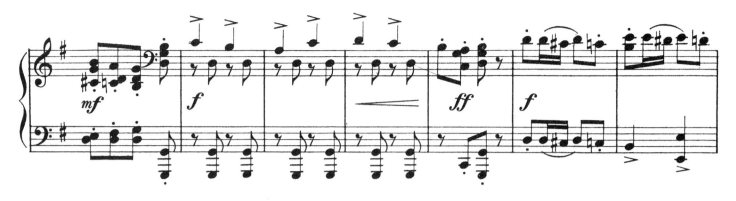

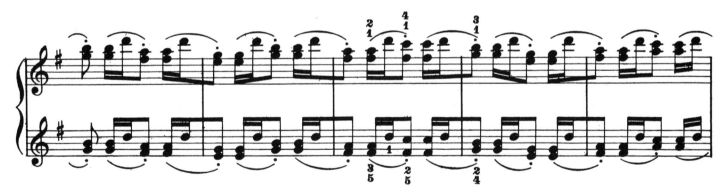

Arab Dance

SECONDO

Arab Dance

PRIMO

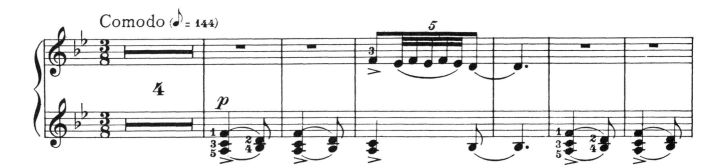

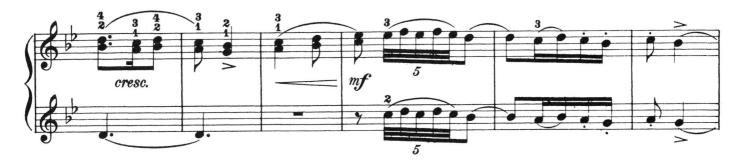

SECONDO

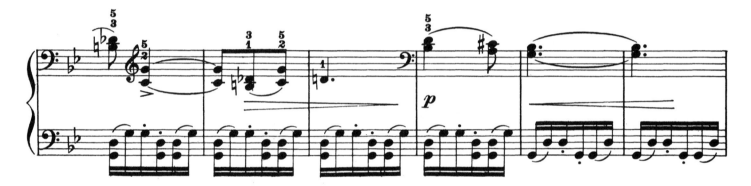

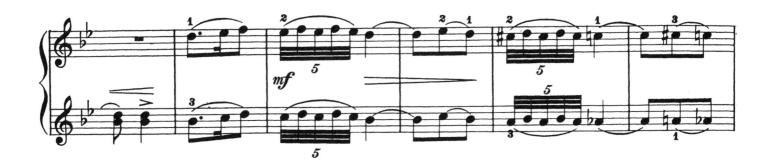

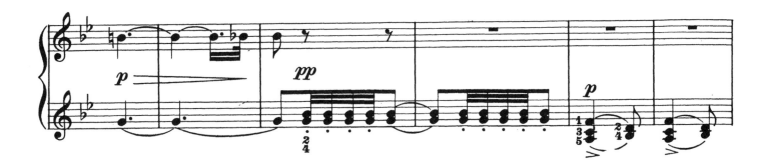

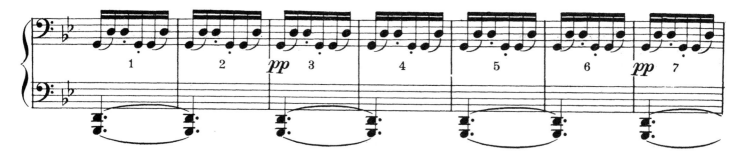

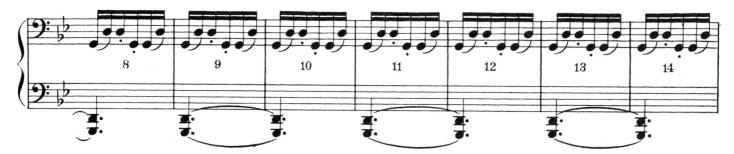

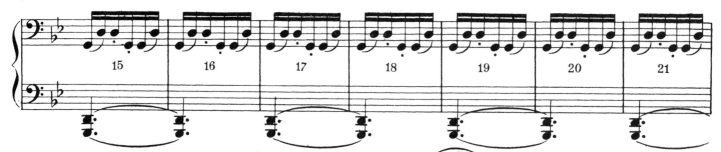

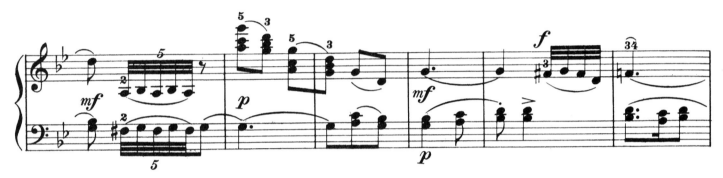

Chinese Dance

SECONDO

Chinese Dance

PRIMO

SECONDO

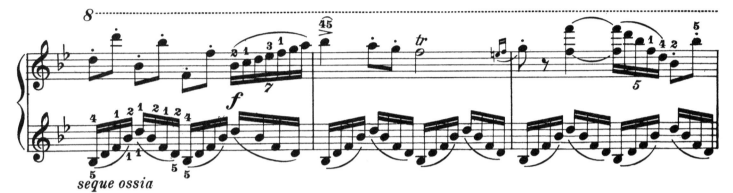

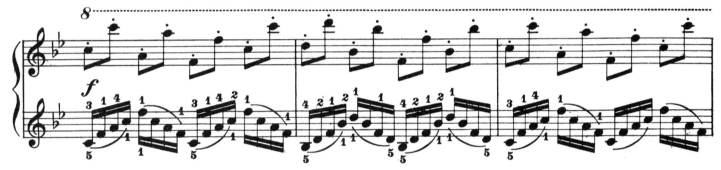

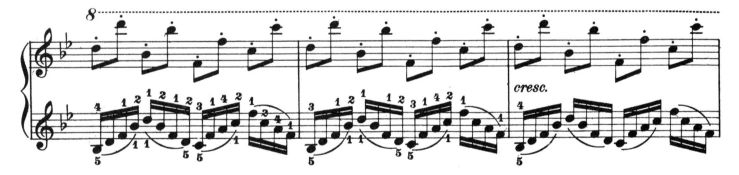

Dance of the Reed-Flutes

SECONDO

Moderato assai (♩ = 76)

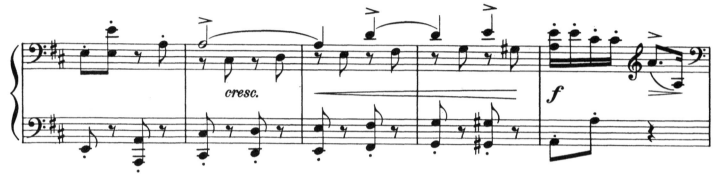

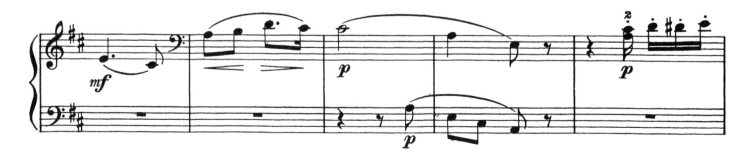

Dance of the Reed-Flutes

PRIMO

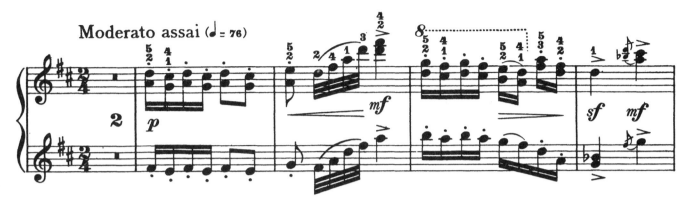

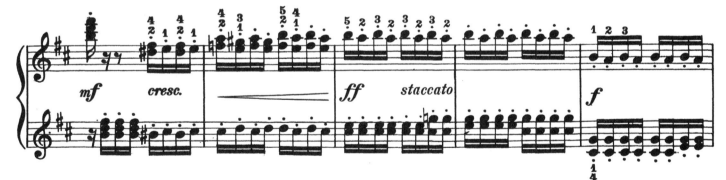

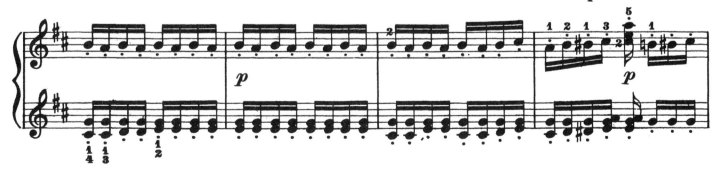

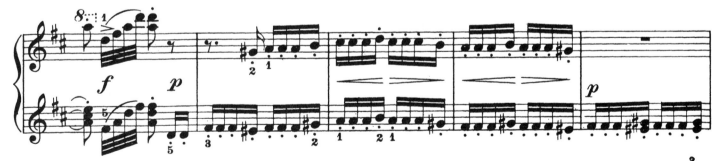

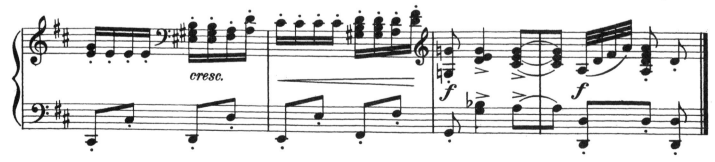

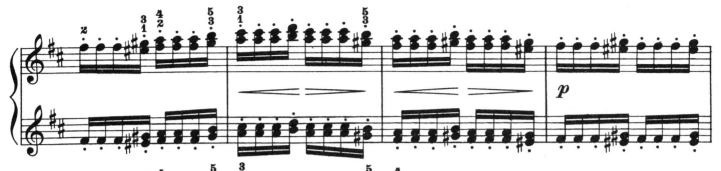

Waltz of the Flowers

SECONDO

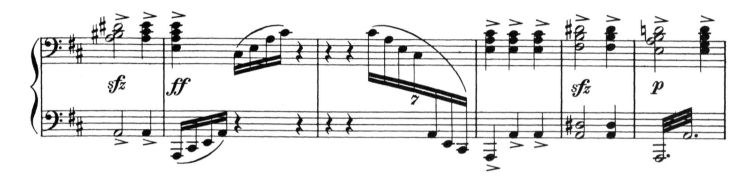

Waltz of the Flowers

PRIMO

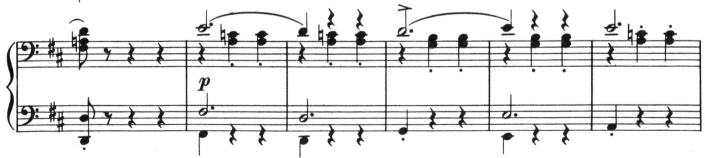

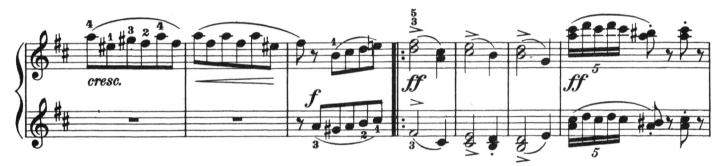

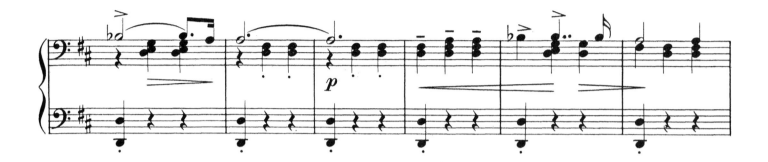

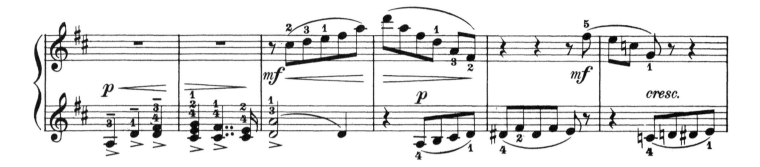

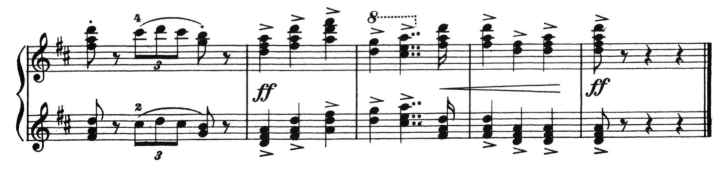